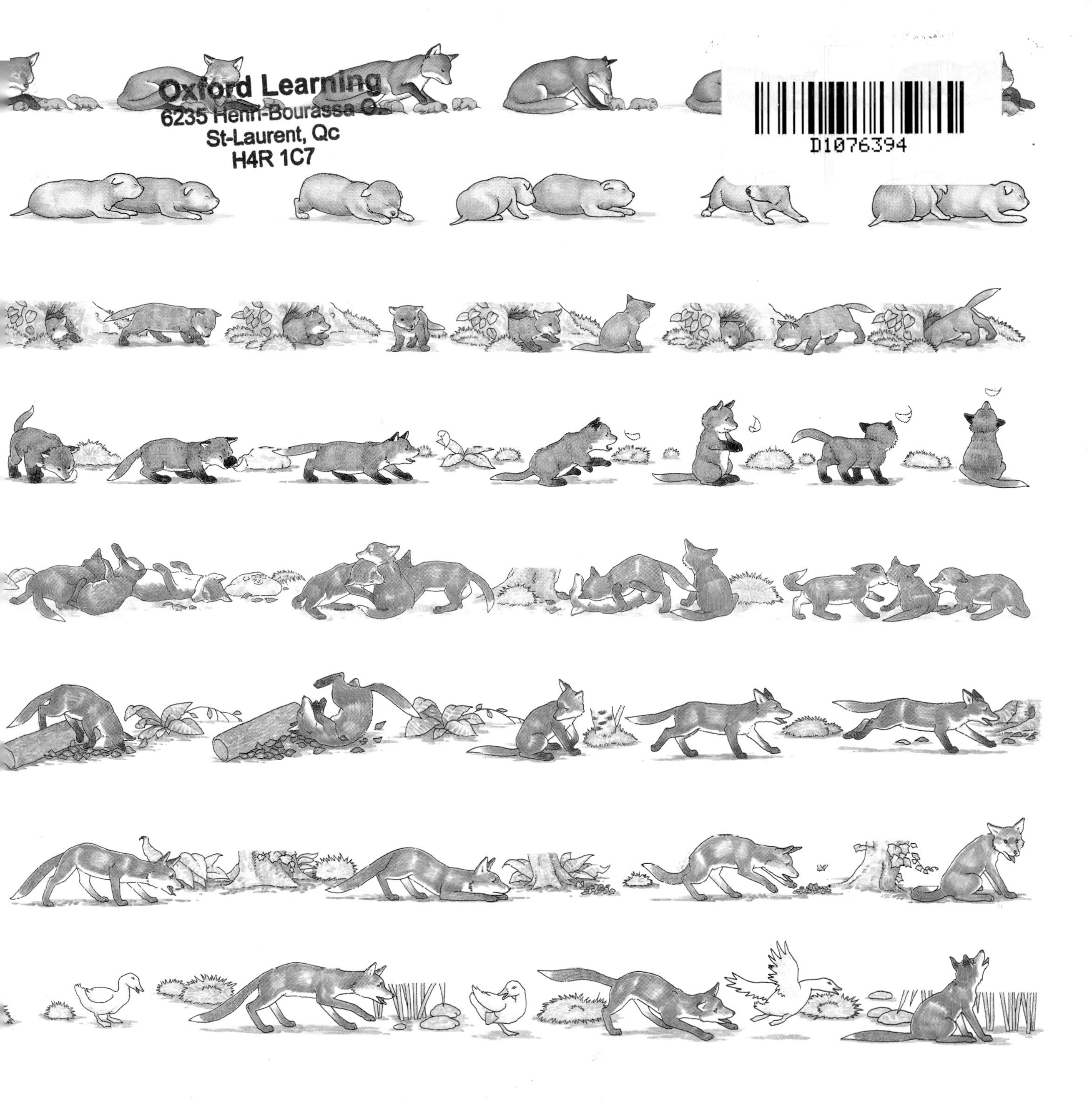

Oxford Learning
6235 Henri-Bourassa O.
St-Laurent, Qc
H4R 1C7
D1076394

A DORLING KINDERSLEY BOOK

Canadian Cataloguing in Publication Data

Burton, Jane
Fox

(See how they grow)
ISBN 0-590-74399-6

1. Foxes – Infancy – Juvenile literature.
2. Foxes - Development – Juvenile literature.
1. Ling, Mary. II . Title. III. Series: See how they grow (Richmond Hill, Ont.).

QL737.C22B87 1992 j599.74'442 C92-093728-4

First published in Canada in 1992 by Scholastic Canada Ltd.
123 Newkirk Road, Richmond Hill, Ontario, L4C 3G5.

Originally published in Great Britain in 1992 by
Dorling Kindersley Limited, 9 Henrietta Street, London WC2E 8PS

Printed in Italy by L.E.G.O. ISBN 0-590-74399-6

Written and edited by Mary Ling
Art Editor Helen Senior
Production Shelagh Gibson
Illustrator Rowan Clifford and Dan Wright

Color reproduction by J. Process Ltd, Singapore

SEE HOW THEY GROW

FOX

photographed by
JANE BURTON

Scholastic Canada Ltd

Brand-new

I was just born. I cannot see or hear, but I can smell.

I can smell my brother and sister close by.

We have downy fur to keep us warm. We sleep most of the time.

This is me.

Snuggling up

I am two weeks old now. My eyes are open and I can see.

This is my mother.
She watches over me while I explore. Where are my brothers and sisters?

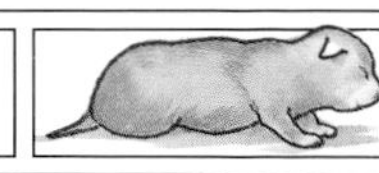

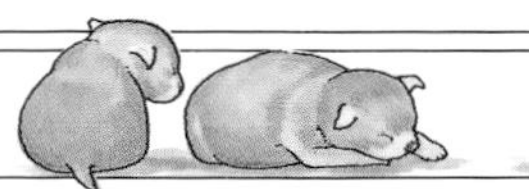

Here they are! It is time for
Mom to feed us
her warm milk.

I am very sleepy
after my dinner.
I snuggle up with
my sister for a nap.

The world outside

I am one month old.
I am growing
bigger every day.

I explore the
world outside our
den. How exciting
it all looks!

I wonder if there are any juicy insects hiding in the grass?

Oh, dear! I have a dirty face. My brother licks it clean before we go home.

Hungry cubs

Now I am six weeks old. My paws and claws are getting bigger.

I am looking for something good to eat.

Oh, no! This eggshell is empty and my nose is stuck!

I hope Mom comes back soon. I am very hungry.

Young hunter

I am eight weeks old. I hear the smallest sounds and I sniff many new smells.

I am a hunter today.
I am tracking my brother.

Here he is! I creep up on him very quietly and jump.

Ouch! That hurts. My brother's teeth are very sharp.

Chasing tails

Now I am ten weeks old. My tail is growing long and bushy.

I love chasing through the woods with the other cubs.

Then I curl up to sleep
in the warm sunshine
with my tail tucked
around me.

Fine red coats

I am twelve weeks old.
My coat is red and
shiny. My legs
are strong.

I find my own
food now. I am
a good hunter.

See how I grew

Newborn

Two weeks old

Four weeks old

Six weeks old

Eight weeks old

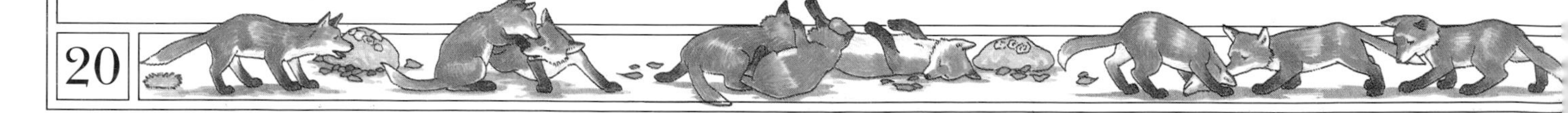

Ten weeks old

Twelve weeks old